Suicide Forest

The Mystery of Aokigahara

True Crime Stories

Roger Harrington

Introduction

At the base of Mount Fuji lies a location with such a dark history that many people consider it too forbidden a topic to discuss. For over 70 years, Aokigahara, Japan has been a source of mystery for both investigators and paranormal researchers. This beautiful stretch of unkempt woodland, while maintaining the illusion of beauty, harbours a secret which few people are willing to acknowledge.

Aokigahara, known to many as the Sea of Trees, is the suicide capital of Japan. Every year, hundreds of people visit the forest with no intention of ever leaving. People who no longer wish to be a part of this world find solace in the isolation of Aokigahara, and willingly take their own lives against its backdrop of chaotic forestry.

However, the legend of Aokigahara goes a lot further that simply being alluring scenery for suicide. Its lore is rooted in ancient legend, literature and a historical association with death. Its impact on Japanese culture has been so prominent that Japanese officials rarely acknowledge the forest's existence in an effort to disassociate it from its macabre infamy. But despite this, Aokigahara's prominence in not just Japanese culture, but world over, cannot be understated.

Aokigahara is known to the world by many names: *the Suicide Forest, the Demon Forest, Black Forest of Death*, but no name embodies its essence more perfectly than the *Sea of Trees.* The forest is incredibly dense, with much of its floor space being covered up by fallen trees, branches, dead vegetation, leaves, sticks, rocks, overgrown shrubbery and moss. The thick undergrowth of the forest makes its surface largely impenetrable, while the thin layers of topsoil forces tree roots to spread across the forest floor like overgrown limbs. The tree coverage is so dense that certain areas of the forest are obscured by darkness before midday. Once inside Aokigahara, getting lost and never returning is a very real possibility even for those without the desire to take their own lives.

Located on the North-facing slope of Mount Fuji, the forest occupies around 35 square kilometres. Its floor, despite now being layered with dense foliage, consists mostly of volcanic rock formed as a result of an eruption of Mount Fuji over a thousand years prior. Over time, this cavern-riddled area of almost-impenetrable volcanic rock became covered with forestry, eventually becoming the Haunted Forest of Death we recognise it as today. There is almost no wildlife to speak of inside Aokigahara, giving off an eerie silence which is only penetrated by the sound of whistling leaves.

Aside from the occasional crow cawing in the distance, Aokigahara is notoriously devoid of sound; an unnaturally silent haven.

Aokigahara can be considered a bridge between reality and the spiritual; at once sacred, accessible, and isolated. Prior to World War 2, it was believed by many was that once a person entered the forest, he or she would be unable to find their way out, trapped in a perpetual twilight, barely able to see the stars or even the peak of Mount Fuji.

Inside Aokigahara, many people report feeling completely isolated, cut-off from society. The forest becomes a surreal netherworld existing outside the everyday human realm, haunted by a persistent, ever-growing history of death, littered with cultural memories of agony and despair.

This belief actually has some basis in science, given the way the forest was originally formed. Due to the igneous nature of the ground, the high iron content creates an area of unusually strong magnetic activity, which makes the forest a challenge to navigate compared to other forests in Japan. It has been shown that within Aokigahara, normal compasses do not function properly due to the abnormally high level of magnetic activity. Based on this geological anomaly, even the Japan Self-Defence Force (the *Jieitai*, or JSDF) admits that commercial navigational tools would be all but useless for someone lost within Aokigahara. This is perhaps something which contributes to the ever growing number of the forest's casualties, whether it was a conscious choice to take their lives or not.

All these elements come together to shape Aokigahara as a place of the lost, the final destination for those seeking to disappear and never be found. Add to this the problematic navigation of the forest, and it becomes clear how the desperate souls who venture to Aokigahara with the intention of committing suicide will not be found until long after their death, assuming they are ever found at all.

A History of Death

Aokigahara's long association with death dates back to ancient times. The act of *ubasute*, which literally translates to 'abandoning a parent', was commonly witnessed by many in Aokigahara in the distant past. *Ubasute* involved taking an elderly relative into a mountain or similar desolate area and simply left there to die. The elderly relative would often by considered an inconvenience by their family, thus making *ubasute* a primitive form of euthanasia. It became prominent during times of hardship; such as amidst droughts or famine. Sacrificing a family member meant that there would be less mouths to feed, ensuring a longer life expectancy for everyone else. A necessary evil in order to perpetuate survival.

It is perhaps because of this ancient practice that the forest has become synonymous with acts of death and despair. Indeed, the legend of *ubasute* commonly occurring inside Aokigahara has speculated theories that the forest remains a purgatory for the restless souls who were left there to die by their families. After all, the deaths suffered by abandoned family members were sure to have been painful, drawn-out deaths brought on by starvation, exposure or dehydration, fuelling beliefs that the forest remains haunted by the spirits of those who were heartlessly abandoned.

Spiritualists further believe that the centuries worth of death, suicide and macabre practices which have taken place inside Aokigahara have tainted the forest's essence. It is considered that the woodland and soil itself has been infused with demonic energy which creates paranormal activity and psychological manipulation inside any of the forest's visitors, whether they harbour suicidal tendencies or not. The twisted tree roots, uneven surfaces and endless winding terrain make it the perfect place to get lost, injured or trapped. It is clear that once inside Aokigahara, something doesn't want you to leave.

The Perfect Place To Die

Forestry workers regular sweep through Aokigahara in order to clean the pathways of unnecessary grit. While on their routine checks, it is not uncommon for workers to come across the possessions of those who have recently decided to end their lives within the confines of the forest, not to mention the bodies themselves. For those undecided as to whether Aokigahara will be their final resting place, they will often take with them possessions in order to persuade or dissuade them of their choice once the moment is upon them.

Workers often report finding teddy bears, diaries, love letters, family photographs, alcohol bottles and jewellery discarded along forest trails, but there are two items in particular which make regular appearances. Two literature works, Tower of Waves by

Seicho Matsumoto (1960), and The Complete Manual of Suicide by Wataru Tsurumi (1993).

Author Seicho Matsumoto released his novel *'Nami no Tou'*, [literally translated as *'Tower Of Waves'*], in which a couple in a doomed relationship make a final trek into Aokigahara for the purpose of ending their lives. Since its publication in 1960, the surge of suicides inside Aokigahara increased greatly, with Japanese governments placing the blame on the romanticising of suicide presented in the novel. Very little is known about the book regarding plot details outside of Japan due to its connotations with Aokigahara and incredibly bleak overtones. It has never been translated into English and has been kept away from the Western world almost entirely for fear of inspiring an entirely new demographic of potential suicide victims.

In 1993, Wataru Tsurumi published a 'self-help' book entitled *The Complete Manual of Suicide.* The book is the most common possession found upon the corpses of suicide victims inside the Suicide Forest. The book; a depressing, nihilistic overview of the monotony of life, was originally meant as a means to educate society on the motivations behind people who choose to take their own lives, and asks readers not to view suicide victims in such a negative light. The opening paragraph claims:

"It's useless to say 'life is dull and boring.' We are all unlucky. We were born on this stage of past events. We will wake at 7 AM, either going to work or going to school afterwards. We will repeat the pointless speeches. At work, we keep saying senseless things while we keep on working over different senseless projects, for a few weeks, a few months or a few years.

New inventions will be introduced at a slow pace. The slow-paced politician will keep on accepting bribes. The TV programs keeps on bringing excitement to its audience at a slow pace. After we switch off the TV, it will be just another ordinary day.

We tolerated the nervousness caused by the terrifying ordinary life, in return for the ridiculous 'calm and bright future.' We have to be careful throughout our life, trying in vain to avoid any mistakes. There's no happy ending like the ones in the comedies. This is the first element leading to suicide."

The book has never been translated to English so details are scarce, however it alludes to Aokigahara as an ideal suicide location as the labyrinthine complexion of the forest is not only a source of terror, but an alluring inspiration for those who have endured the struggles of living in the modern world. According to *The Complete*

Manual of Suicide, Aokigahara is "the perfect place to die".

Dignity in Death

Japan's suicide rates are far higher than any other wealthy country. On average, around 70 people a day take their own lives. It is certainly a prominent theme in Japan; it is a go-to solution when all else seems to fail.

In order to understand the prominence of 'suicide culture', we must first understand the embedded notion of 'person removal'. Japanese media will often cover stories on a CEO making a bad business decision and thus stepping down from his position. Sports coaches may lose an important game, to which he may fire himself and thusly end his own career.

Or, a *salaryman* (Japanese equivalent of a white collar worker) may feel he is worth more to the world dead, and step out in front of a train.

In Japanese culture, suicide plays a different role than it does in Western civilisation. In the West, suicide is often considered 'cowardly' or 'selfish', whereas Japan has maintained a different view for several centuries. *Seppuku,* a form of ritual suicide was embedded in Japan's samurai code as a way for warriors to retain honour upon their capture by the enemy. To avoid torture or imprisonment, the samurai would often disembowel himself with his sword before the chance of capture presented itself, and was considered a justified response to failure or inevitable defeat in battle. The purpose being to release the warrior's spirit and thus avoid any possibility of a dishonourable death at the hands of an enemy.

It is perhaps because of this honourable tradition that Japan's suicide rate is the highest in the world. Where many civilisations see suicide as a sin, Japan sees it as a way of "taking responsibility", or even a form of macabre respect.

Japanese culture values the notion of "collective thinking" – the idea that individual identities should be sacrificed for the benefit of conformity and acceptance - above any form of individuality. Being shunned by others is often conceived as a punishment worse than death.

This, therefore seeks to denounce any form of uniqueness by painting it as something to be discarded or looked down upon. Children who don't fit in at school, recluses, people who enjoy uncommon activities – these are the types of people who Japanese society has been programmed to consciously cast aside. When this is combined with loneliness or financial troubles (the two biggest motivations for suicide), it becomes clear why taking one's own life could become an alluring prospect.

Despite the more tolerant views and social acceptability of suicide in Japan, the rate of growth of suicide is still a cause for concern. In particular, the growing phenomenon of *shinju,* [translated: *suicide pacts]. Shinju* has been reported to have occurred multiple times in Aokigahara, often with the pact being agreed on internet forums and message boards beforehand. They are usually formed of a group of strangers who all share the same desire to end their lives.

It is important to note that these suicide pacts have not been as well-accepted by society as honour suicide due to there being no element of sacrifice involved. *Sepukku* serves a purpose, whereas *shinju* is considered an impulsive and reckless act. Or, what is more likely, is that *shinju* serves a great purpose for those involved, yet their motives are unclear to anyone *not* suffering from the profound loneliness they feel.

There is a unique beauty in this; strangers who bond over the longing to die. After all, it is likely the feeling of them not belonging to any collective in the first place which would prompt them to seek out like-minded individuals.

Aokigahara appears to be related to this Japanese notion of self-sacrifice as an act of heroism for several reasons. First of all, when a person decides to end their life by jumping in front of a train at a busy station, it would not be considered a form of self-sacrifice by the rest of the world. It would be cause an incredible inconvenience for hundreds of people, not to mention the possible trauma it could inflicting on unwilling spectators. By committing suicide in a place like Aokigahara, a person is removing themselves from society as silently as possible. The only people who would discover their bodies are people who expect to be discovering bodies, or at the very least, someone who wouldn't be shocked to find a suicide victim in a location famous for suicides.

Secondly, a person who makes the pilgrimage to the Suicide Forest to end their lives is not only conveniencing the people who might witness his or her death, but they are also making their intentions clear. They are telling their family and friends: *"I came here for the purpose of dying"*. It proves their willingness to die for the greater good. It says that their decision was not made lightly and it was not made impulsively. They knowingly set out to make life better for everyone else by taking their own.

Suicide Through Silence

Reportage writer Ramu Murata has been to the Suicide Forest over 30 times with his work. He claims that some of the most disturbing sites he's ever seen have been inside Aokigahara, and while he's seen a lot, some visuals still manage to unnerve him.

In January 2008, Murata came across a decaying old truck abandoned deep inside the forest. There was no body to speak of, either in the truck or in the surrounding area, but it looked like it had been lived in for a decent amount of time.

"People will hibernate in [their vehicles] or tents if they've arrived at their destination but are still hesitant to go through with the act. I imagine it takes a lot of courage to end your own life."

The truck Murata found was surrounded by wooden Buddha statues and of pictures of *kamisama ('Gods')*. There were no roads nearby, so the method of how the truck arrived at this particular spot was a mystery to Murata.

"It was such a shock to come across, it didn't feel real. It was like a horror movie. When something horrific is in a completely mundane place; somewhere it shouldn't be - but was. I felt like my heart was going to stop'.

Abandoned vehicles are an incredibly common, albeit distressing sight around the forest. Murata has claimed there is no more a saddening image than a car covered in ice, leaves and snow; clearly having been in its spot for longer than its neighbouring counterparts, while life continues to go on regardless.

Mutara claims it is a fitting metaphor for the Japanese cultural response to suicide; to greet it with cold silence.

All forms of mental illness are heavily stigmatised in Japan. There is no real outlet for help for anyone suffering from schizophrenia, personality disorders, or indeed suicidal thoughts. While the Western world view mental illness as something which is out of a person's control, the Japanese perception of abnormal psychology is that it has been caused by character flaws, errors in their personality or them simply choosing to be different.

Most people who commit suicide do so by entering Aokigahara from the wind cave and ice caves. But because many come at night and it's almost impossible to traverse into the forest from the path that connects the two caves. Many commit suicide within tens of metres of the path, therefore it is not uncommon for tourists to come across discarded possessions, vehicles and even bodies in the way that Mutara did.

He once found a driving license with the face and address of the owner burnt away; a symbolic representation of a person who would soon no longer be part of this world. There are lots of these 'graphic remainders' spread throughout the forest. Mutara once found a cassette tape along with some shoes on the spot of a suicide. He thought it might contain a will or last testament so he took it home to play.

But when Mutara turned it on - it was classical musical.

"When I think that they must have listened to this when they were dying. I just didn't know what to think. I remember just putting my hands together in prayer."

Recently, he was travelling with friends along the route 139 when they saw a suited man entering the forest holding hands with a small child. The child look distressed, and the situation looked completely unnatural for something occurring so early in the morning. Mutara does not know what happened to them.

"As much as I'd like to, it's not my place to inquire. There could have been a million reasons why they were going in there together. But why would I ask? In Japan we have an emphasis on over-politeness as well as 'don't ask, don't tell' culture, especially regarding people's personal lives. It was simply another mystery lost inside the Suicide Forest."

The pair could have been visiting the forest for educational purposes, or they could have been preparing to end their lives there. There have since been reports of sightings of an old man and young girl who walk in hand-in-hand through the forest at night, however it is likely not the departed souls of these people (this event is covered in a later chapter – *The Old Man And The Girl)*.

The Hangman's Trail

Stories of singular hauntings inside Aokigahara are common. Individual accounts of persons witnessing a lone apparition appearing or dispersing from sight tally up into the thousands. However, the story of the Hangman's Trail suggests a different type of force at work inside Aokigahara; a force which imbues the energy of the entire forest as one collective, malevolent entity.

In July 2010, British-born criminology student David Reed, visited the Suicide Forest in an attempt to, like many other curious visitors, come across any morbid paraphernalia relating to suicide or death. According to accounts from his girlfriend at the time, Reed had two motivations for obtaining such trophies.

One, Reed wanted to impress his girlfriend with his adventurous spirit, and two, Reed was very interested in the trade of 'murderabilia' – the buying and selling of items relating to true crime incidents. It is a taboo trade mostly associated with America and Europe, so Reed was likely interested in being one of the first people in the Asian-speaking world to embrace it.

According to Reed's girlfriend (who undertook the same criminology course as him at the time), Reed had been in contact with a Japanese murderer for the purposes of his studies, however, their relationship had progressed to the point that they remained in regular correspondence. Although the inmate (who cannot be legally referred to by name due to the unofficial nature of his statements) had only been convicted of one murder, he revealed in a letter to Reed that he had previously killed another victim and hidden his corpse within the depths of

Aokigahara. His letter [translated from Japanese] detailed the following:

"When you reach the sign [which] says 'consult the police before you choose to die', don't go down that path. Take a left and head straight through the trees. Keep going until [you arrive at a] small clearing. There's a tree covered in yellow industrial tape. The [Hangman's] Trail starts there. I dumped him somewhere along there. Don't take it as gospel though. His body might have been moved. They [authorities] probably assumed he overdosed or something."

Some Japanese sources say that "The Hangman" is the essence of Aokigahara in living form. There is a clear relationship between the forest and the idolisation of the noose. Sprawled along the forest floors, overgrown weeds and branches curl and knot themselves as though they are imitating the object which is the catalyst to so many deaths. There is a force at work; a supernatural energy which has manifested from centuries of misery inside Aokigahara.

The Hangman's Trail earned its name due to it being the death site of nine foreigners over the years, all of them considered to be tourists by authorities. Their deaths (and indeed, their possessions) indicated that they were simply visiting the forest for tourist purposes. This suggests that these nine men had no intention of making Aokigahara their final resting place, yet were all found hanged along a specific 1.5km stretch of forestry.

David Reed entered the forest on the afternoon of Sunday 25th July, 2010. His communication with his girlfriend indicated that he was there until at least 5pm. The messages between the two suggested that Reed had discovered possessions of previous suicide victims and, while hadn't taken them as mementos, had taken pictures of the items he found.

There was no additional communication between the two until 10:30pm, when Reed's girlfriend received a message saying simply: "Lost".

She immediately alerted officials that Reed was missing somewhere in the depths of the forest. A search was undertaken the same evening, however there would be no sight of David Reed until August 10th, 2010.

The body of David Reed was discovered during a routine sweep by forest officials. Strangely, he had not died of exhaustion or exposure to the elements as was considered at the time. Reed was found hanging from a tree branch as though he had willingly taken his own life.

Reed's girlfriend states that he harboured no suicidal tendencies, ruling out the possibility that his reasoning for going into the forest was simply a ruse in order to carry out his true agenda. However, the possessions of

David Reed tell a different story. In particular, the contents of his phone.

Reed's possessions were discovered underneath a pile of rocks around 10 yards from where he was found hanged. While it is true that Reed was telling his girlfriend the truth when he said he taken photographs of suicide victim's possessions, it came to light that the only photographs recently taken were of his Reed's own items, perhaps an introverted way of telling his girlfriend the truth without having to be straightforward with her.

Paranormal enthusiasts have theorised that David Reed did indeed become lost inside Aokigahara, and subsequently became the tenth known victim of the apparition known as the Hangman. While not considered to be a restless spirit of someone who once died in Aokigahara, the Hangman is believed to be the embodiment of the forest's malignity, suggesting that suicides are no longer enough to satisfy its need for sorrow; that it needs to invoke unwilling deaths in order to remain fulfilled.

Theories regarding the fate of David Reed differ extensively. His demeanour pointed to a well-adjusted young male with no suicidal thoughts and simply visited the Black Forest out of morbid curiosity. Some evidence, however, suggests Reed paid a visit to Aokigahara with no intention of coming out.

There is, of course, a distinct possibility that while Reed did not visit the forest for the purposes of ending his life, he felt compelled to offer his life by the vengeful presences at work inside Aokigahara.

Art Imitates Death

Although fiction offers the possibility of endless circumstances conjured up by an artist's imagination, reality is made all the more terrifying by the simple fact it has not been envisioned, but simply *came to be.* As with the works of literature which have inspired many to end their lives within Aokigahara, this is an example of Oscar Wilde's famous quote coming to fruition; art imitating life, life imitating art.

While it is true Aokigahara's timeless association with death transcends any possible measurement, the notoriety of the forest increased upon its fictional depictions. *Tower of Waves,* the 1960 novel by Seicho Matsumoto, alludes to Aokigahara as an already established place to commit suicide. Even by 1960, Aokigahara's history as a burial ground for abandoned elderly relatives was well established. Art imitating life.

Upon its fictionalisation, many lonely and depressed souls similar to the book's protagonist would flock to the forest in order to emulate her demise, adding fuel to the fire of the forest's real-world prominence. Its reputation as a gateway to death establishing itself even further, cementing it's synonymy with suicide for the modern age. Life imitating art.

Fictional portrayals of Aokigahara continue to materialise, but it is at the point which fiction and reality overlap that it becomes something unlike anywhere else in the world. The case of seventeen year old student, Miyako Nagai, one of the youngest known victims found inside Aokigahara, perfectly embodies this strange phenomenon.

In May 2011 (exact dates remain unknown), Miyako Nagai entered Aokigahara alone with the intention of ending her life. Nagai headed deep into the woodland, purposely getting herself lost so that she was unlikely to return even if she had wanted to. Once suitably desolate, Nagai overdosed on sleeping pills and collapsed to the ground.

Once reported missing, investigations into Nagai's disappearance uncovered a strange obsession she had with the Suicide Forest. At her parents' home, police uncovered a diary detailing fictional accounts of events inside Aokigahara, as well as illustrations and poems about what it would be like to take one's own life there.

Without surprise, Nagai's body was discovered two weeks later by authorities in a remote western part of the forest. Much like other suicides, Nagai had taken her most important items on her final journey; one of which was torn pages from her diary. A fictionalisation of her final moments, written an unknown period of time prior to her death.

[Transcribed from the diary of Miyako Nagai. Translated from Japanese]:

Meisa was a horror enthusiast. While other girls asked for Barbies and lip gloss, she would pester her parents for a Chucky doll, or money to buy a scary costume, even months before Halloween began to cross people's minds.

Meisa and her best friend, Ikki, loved to visit creepy places. Abandoned mansions, cemeteries, asylums. The Suicide Forest, to the pair, is the holy grail of haunted places.

"Cmon Meisa, cheer up!" demanded Ikki.

"Ikki. I'm not going to keep repeating myself," replied Meisa. "There's no way I'm going in there."

Meisa hadn't always acted like Shaggy from Scooby Doo. But ever since a freak car accident, she'd become sullen and introverted. Even convincing her to go with him to see the forest had been a challenge for Ikki. Now they'd made it this far, he wasn't going to let her ruin this.

"Whatever," snapped Ikki. "Just follow closely behind."

They arrived at the entrance as the darkness of the evening was beginning to stake its claim on the forest. Before taking their first steps inside, they noticed a sign written in Japanese. A plea to tourists, urging them not to end their lives. The sign added to the atmosphere perfectly.

Ikki turned to Meisa:

"Once we start trekking, you'll notice how dense the trees are, and that much of the floor is covered in volcanic rock. In theory, I can see how someone could find the forest unnerving. The problem we have, however, is our proximity to civilization.

The noise of the cars speeding across the nearby road will undoubtedly ruin the eerie vibe the trees might have created."

Ikki continued:

"But, of course, the main appeal lies in wandering off the trail; maybe we could try to reach the icy caves nearby. We could mark our trail with tape to make sure we don't get lost. The trek will be difficult, because there are overturned trees everywhere. There isn't a single patch of level ground."

They had been walking for what felt to them like a few kilometres, when the darkness started to noticeably increase.

"So... what do you think?" asked Meisa.

"It's really not scary at all," replied Ikki. "I's love to be able to fill my diary with vivid descriptions of how unnerving the place is, but really, all I can say is that it's a damn beautiful forest."

"Well, I think it's pretty scary," offered Meisa.

"I know you do."

A few more minutes passed. Ikki called to his friend.

"Hey Meisa, you've been far too quiet. Everything okay?"

Meisa's reply was unexpected. "You don't hear them? The voices?" she whispered. Ikki turned round and saw his friend was unquestionably frightened.

"You're kidding, right?"

Ikki was surprised that Meisa would be susceptible to this. "It's your imagination. You're only hearing voices because of the constant exposure to horror tropes. It gets to you, and your mind starts inventing things to fit the atmosphere. There is litera-"

"What the hell is that?!" cried Meisa, pointing straight ahead. It looked like the shape of a person a little way ahead. Unsettling maybe, but far from horrific. People went camping in this forest all the time.

"Hello! Can you hear me?" Ikki called to the figure.

"Oh? There's someone else here?" the figure replied. "Yes, hold on, I'm coming over."

As he came closer, he was revealed to the pair as an elderly western man, with a tired but kind face. Shaking hands with ikki, he introduced himself as Mr. William Wood. Ikki accepted the handshake, partly as a greeting, and partly to reassure Meisa that they weren't dealing with a ghostly apparition. In the conversation that followed, Ikki and Meisa learned their fellow traveller had survived cancer, and was now set on exploring the world. They made idle chit-chat, but Mr Wood's attention was diverted by Meisa, who still looked terrified.

"You heard them, didn't you?" he asked her. "The voices?"

"Yes! Yes I did!" Meisa almost yelled. "I can hear them now. It's as if they're calling me, telling me to come closer…"

"What on Earth are you two talking about?" Ikki interrupted, the frustration clear in his voice. "Look Mr. Wood, I'd be grateful if you didn't help my friend scare herself."

"We aren't making this up, Ikki," Meisa insisted. "We really are hearing voices."

Ikki ignored her, turning his attention to the old man. "What are you doing here anyway?" Ikki decided that assertiveness was the best policy. "If you're intending to do something to yourself, I'm afraid I'll have to call the police."

"No, no… I'm sorry," stuttered Mr Wood. "I didn't mean to cause any trouble. I'm just out *here camping." There was no insincerity in his expression.*

"Whatever. Come on Meisa." Ikki turned to leave, his friend following grudgingly.

The walk back was uneventful; Still upset with each other, a resentful silence hung over Meisa and Ikki. The tape markings they'd made led the way back to the main path, and from there they returned to the car. Ikki hated being at odds with his best friend; he knew he should say something, offer an olive branch.

"He heard us."

"What?" Meisa was clearly still irritated.

"He heard what we said about the voices. That's why he claimed to have heard them himself. He was messing with you; it was obvious you were scared and he was playing on that."

"I heard them!" Meisa insisted. "I can't believe you're dismissing this as if it's nothing! High

pitched sing-song voices trying to get me to go to them. They were there, clear as day!"

"Listen to yourself, you've ruined this whole thing!" Screamed Ikki. "Ever since your stupid accident, all you've done is let your emotions cloud your judgement! You're not capable of being level hea-"

There was a deafening thud. The car had hit something.

"Shit!"

The day just keeps getting worse and worse, thought Ikki.

They got out of the car and found they'd hit A tanuki, a Japanese raccoon dog that had made its way onto the road and out in front of their car.

Ikki stared at the lifeless body. "Shit, man. Look at it. Such a cute thing, all mangled. It's screwing with my head. And this is coming from someone with a high tolerance for messed up shit."

Meisa's eyes widened. "It heard them. It heard the voices and threw itself in front of our car."

She was inconsolable for the rest of the jourmey to the hotel. Ikki's mood wasn't much better, so the drive passed in relative silence. They went to their respective rooms without a word.

A few hours later, Meisa received a text from Ikkki:

"Look, I'm still convinced the whole thing was a coincidence. But still, I don't want to be on my own tonight. Will you keep me company?"

Meisa stared at the message, and then her fingers were a blur as she composed a reply:

"Ikki? You mean..."

"Just get up here."

The next morning saw them in drastically better spirits. The journey to the airport was pleasant, enhanced by their excitement at the thought of going home. They agreed that once they arrived back, they'd take a break from all the horror stuff for a while.

Ikki noticed with some annoyance that he and Meisa weren't sitting together on the plane. "Why don't we ask whoever's next to you to swap? We could tell them we're a couple; we wouldn't really be lying…"

Meisa beamed at him in reply.

But, as their luck would have it, there was a mother and daughter sitting next to Ikki. "It's fine," Meisa shrugged. "We'll figure it out during the layover." Her seat was at the other end of the plane; she kissed him and left for the front. The mother and daughter, noisy and irritating, finally got seated beside Ikki. He put on his headphones and blocked out the humdrum *around him, starting to doze almost immediately…*

When Ikki woke up, an hour had passed. He decided to visit Meisa at the front, using the bathroom nearby as an excuse to meet. Squishing past the mother and daughter, Ikki strode eagerly up the plane to see his new girlfriend.

Meisa's seat was empty.

Ikki found a passing flight attendant and asked where Meisa was.

"She left the plane ten minutes before take-off."

Ikki hurried back to his seat. He knew where she'd gone. He could stop her, he knew he could; when had she ever not listened to him? Pausing only to pay for the in-flight wifi, he took out his phone to send her a message.

His phone buzzed before he could type anything. Meisa had sent a text as soon as she'd left the plane:

"I need to tell you something. A confession, I guess. When I had that accident, and I was inches from having my life snatched away, I heard voices then, too. Except, well, the voices weren't the same then. Those voices were dark, malicious. But they were still taunting me, still calling me to join them.

And then, for a fleeting a moment, I saw it: the dark place the voices came from. There was a burning in the pit of my stomach, like I was always doomed to go back to that place one day.

That old man, Mr Wood - he heard those voices too, when he was ill. The tanuki heard them. But the voices in the forest were... different somehow. Calming, childlike. Those voices were welcoming me; it felt like they were offering me sanctuary. I had to go with them. I'm so sorry.

Dying in Aokigahara is the only chance you get to die without going to the dark place.

END.

In this story, Meisa is considered to be Nagai, while the identity of Ikki remains a mystery. Nagai had no close male friends in her real life, so this is perhaps the reason for this fictional creation. It is additionally likely that Nagai painted herself as the secondary character due to the inferiority she felt in the real world. In Nagai's possessions found at her home, she had alluded to both 'voices' and 'sanctuaries' several times in her journals, and was confirmed to have been in a car accident in her younger years.

It is believed that Miyako Nagai did indeed suffer from delusions which drew her towards Aokigahara. Whether this was caused via a cognitive irregularity, a supernatural force, or a severe longing for solace in death is still, and will likely remain, unknown forever.

Eyes of a Death God

There is a classic trope in literature which addresses the idea of witnessing something so unfathomable that the only logical recourse is madness.

In Japanese folklore, a *shinigami* is a supernatural figure relating to death. As per the ominous figure of the Grim Reaper in Western cultures, the shinigami is the Japanese equivalent. For a human being to lay eyes on a shinigami is considered unheard of unless special circumstances allow for it. To witness such a legendary apparition in the flesh would drive a person to insanity due to the incomprehensible knowledge imparted on them.

While the Western world considers the Grim Reaper a singular figure who serves as the personification of Death itself, the Asian world holds regards death as less of an individual to be feared and more of a natural part of the cycle of life. The *shinigami,* then, can be considered as assistants who ensure the smooth transition between life and death.

Shinigami's association with Aokigahara throughout the decades has been well documented. Some paranormal investigators even believe that the whole forest may be a sanctuary for *shinigami* to exist on earth, and serves as gateway between our world and the afterlife.

Sightings of *shinigami* in the forest are plentiful, but a particular incident occurred between an American couple in May 2009 which involved a man claiming a *shinigami* took the life of his partner. Chris and Dawn Tinsley paid a visit to the forest to celebrate their anniversary, but only Chris would come home.

Dawn is believed to have willingly ended her life in Aokigahara, although Chris

Tinsley's statement to the American police paints a different story. It came to light after the investigation that Chris suffered from mild schizophrenia which often erupted during stressful periods of his life, however, police ruled his wife's death as a suicide possibly out of convenience.

Chris's story has since been fictionalised using his official statement as the framework:

"my wife and I had always been passionate about the Japan and its culture; actually, it was something we bonded over when we first met. So for our five year anniversary, we decided to make the trip.

After about a week of planning, we made arrangements to spend 3 days in the Yamanashi Prefecture, in the countryside right next to Mt. Fuji.

We flew over to Tokyo, took a train over to the city of Fujiyoshida, and from there we took a taxi to Narusawa, the village where we'd be staying. On the train, Dawn asked me if I was interested in visiting Aokigahara, a place I'd never heard of, in all honesty. She explained that Aokigahara was a forest at the base of Mt. Fuji, famous for being a disturbingly popular spot for suicides. Hearing the whole suicide thing sort of freaked me out, but I went along with it since her eagerness to visit was written all over her face.

We stayed at a local ryokan – a traditional Japanese inn with hot spring baths, futons instead of beds, that whole thing. In the ryokan, patrons usually get an assigned waitress for the duration of their stay, meaning that all the time you're there you'll probably only interact with one waitress. We got the head waitress, since her knowledge of some English meant better communication with us.

The day we arrived, we were so exhausted we spent most of the afternoon resting in our room. A little while before sunset, we went for a walk around the block. The contrast of old-style houses with modern vending machines and ATMs was fascinating. Near to the ryokan, there was a lookout point, and from what we could make out, it had a fantastic view of the area, from Mt. Fuji all the way down to Saiko Lake. Dawn was thrilled at this discovery, and asked to go there.

I was so tired, all I wanted was dinner and sleep. I wanted to tell her that we'd go the next day, but you know how it is. Your lover's pleading face at sunset could persuade you to do just about anything.

When we got up to the lookout point, the twilight had already turned to night. The view was great, just like we'd expected. We gazed out over a huge expanse of the Japanese countryside we loved so much, and us standing there together, just enjoying the scenery was an unforgettable moment for me.

One of the features dominating the landscape was Aokigahara; its contours were illuminated by tiny buildings and lampposts dotted along the road, but the view grew darker the further inward you looked. At that moment, I became aware of spinning around in place, trying to take in every single nook and cranny. My wife, however, wouldn't take her eyes from the forest.

"Snap out of it," I joked. Her face remained serene, almost melancholic. She spun round to face me:

"Let's go to Aokigahara right now."

But this was one request too many. It was dark, I was exhausted, and the thought of going inside a famous suicide forest wasn't an enchanting idea to me. She kept insisting, I kept refusing. Eventually we both found ourselves walking back towards the ryokan, the mood gone sour.

Some ryokan rooms have their own outdoor hot spring baths, but ours was the more traditional kind with two common baths – one for the men, and one for the women. Still bitter about our earlier disagreement, I told Dawn I'd go to the bath before dinner, and suggested she might like to do the same. She agreed, and we went our separate ways. Half an hour later I went back to our room and found it empty. I assumed Dawn was still in the bath, but a moment later the head maid came in and handed me a neatly folded piece of paper. In broken but understandable English, she explained that she'd received instructions from Dawn to deliver the note to me as soon as I returned from my bath.

I read the note: "I went there anyway."

I ran outside. I was furious with her, but that was overshadowed by worry. Despite the whole creepy suicide forest story, I was mostly concerned was that she was alone at night, an outsider in a strange country. Finding Aokigahara wasn't difficult, since there were signs pointing the way all over the streets, but the walk from the ryokan still took about half an hour. I ran like my life depended on it. I reached the entrance to the forest, an imposing wall of trees, in about 15 minutes.

I'm not ashamed to say it took all I had to muster up enough courage to enter Aokigahara, but I did it, hell bent as I was on finding my wife.

At the time, I didn't know that it was common for suicidal people inside Aokigahara to tie a rope to a tree at the entrance and drag it along as they went deeper in. I guess it was a safety net of sorts - if they had second thoughts, they could find their way out again.

My only source of light was my phone. I could barely make out a thing in there; the place was claustraphobic. I kept coming across different ropes twisting and turning in every direction; any of them could have led to a body. Add the abandoned sets of camping equipment tossed around on the ground, and it was probably the most terrifying thing I had ever witnessed.

I know the police make regular searches, and volunteers remove the bodies from the forest, but I found out first-hand how these corpses are discovered - following the ropes and the putrid smell.

The deeper I got into the forest, the worse things became. I discovered hanged bodies, lightly swaying in the branches. I found decomposing bodies inside ruined tents. The air was cloying, damp and suffocating. The impenetrable darkness made me second guess myself, and what I thought I saw. But the smell... I vomited as I came across my third corpse. I guess the rotting stench and the fear got the better of me.

There was no way of knowing if I Dawn was nearby. I was wandering in random directions, frightened to even call her name. Suddenly I heard leaves cracking somewhere over to the left, and gingerly followed the sound. I found a rope -

one end was fastened to a nearby tree, the other disappeared into the darkness inside the forest. It was twisting and jerking, as if someone were pulling it from the other end. Someone must have been at the other end of the rope, and it could very well have been her.

Something else I didn't know about Aokigahara was its ancient reputation for spirituality.

I followed this rope, which had now become my hope and guiding light Somehow, clinging onto the rope made me feel safer, like she must have been on the other end. By now, the deeper I went the fewer bodies I found. Everyone who'd made it to this point had already done the deed, or they'd changed their minds. The rope was steadying, like I was close to the end of it.

That's when the voice rang out:

"I thought you loved me."

"You told me we were meant to be."

-'Wasn't I good enough?'

"How could you do this to me?"

The trees, the air, my mind – the voice seemed to come from everywhere, her accusations taunting me. I quickened my pace, even more desperate to find Dawn. To apologize to her.

"I knew all along."

"I thought you'd stop."

By now I was sprinting to the end of the rope. Finally, I could just make out a human figure, silhouetted in the far-off darkness. As I neared the figure, I began to know it was her.

But she wasn't alone.

The shinigami death gods of Japanese folklore are usually portrayed as disfigured, pale white beings with humanoid features. They are often depicted carrying some kind of blade, like a knife or a scythe, similar to western portrayals of the Grim

Reaper. The creature grabbing my wife's hair with its cracked, decaying hands was just like the pictures I'd seen in books. The fear and shock was so overwhelming that at first I didn't notice it only held her head. The rest of Dawn's body lay at the creature's feet, severed cleanly at the neck.

It began to walk towards me, still holding my wife's head, each step looking contorted and painful. Grabbing the rope I'd used as a guide, I turned around and ran like my life depended on it. At that moment, I think it did.

In shock, I managed to find my way out of the forest. I begged the few people I came across on the surrounding roads for help, but there was too much of a language barrier for me to be understood. Even so, it was clear to them that I was scared and panicked, and the police were called.

The police didn't speak English, so they fetched the only person in the village who did, which turned out to be our maid from the ryokan.

Exhaustion had forced me to calm down somewhat, so I was able to describe to the maid the events I'd just witnessed. The expression on her face as she listened was perplexing. She turned and addressed the police and others in Japanese. They talked among themselves, the expressions on their faces mirroring each other. Eventually she turned to me again:

"We never talk about that. We leave it alone."

The case was reported as another suicide, the latest in a long list. Explaining the truth to our family and friends was impossible. From that day, I had to go along with the story of her suicide, even during her funeral. I've never been able to understand why I heard those voices inside Aokigahara. For months I'd assumed it was nothing more than an hallucination, brought on by terror.

This morning, however, as I was doing some housework, I found a letter behind one of our *picture frames. It was a suicide note; the first line read:*

"I know you're cheating on me."

END.

The geographical details in this fictionalisation are factually accurate. The only unconfirmed details of the story are in the final section - Chris' account of seeing the figure of a *shinigami* in the flesh, a claim that very few people have ever made.

What We Leave Behind

"Life seems to be a black and white silent movie about nothing, flickering silently on film superimposed onto the retinas of my eyes."

These were the handwritten final words of a man who committed suicide in Aokigahara in 2007. A message to a world he felt he no longer belonged to. Suicide notes are extremely common in Aokigahara, many of them expressing disdain or contempt for life's futility. Some of them apologising, some taking comfort in the fact they won't ever have to face life's meaningless trivialities ever again.

It's difficult to not imagine how a person's final moments might play out, especially given the objects often found amongst suicide victims' possessions. Reports claim to regularly find mundane objects like batteries, cigarettes, lipstick, toothpaste, toothbrushes, umbrellas. A particular famous image of a makeshift grave in Aokigahara shows a person's ID card, torn to shreds and discarded at the base of their resting place. It often seems that a person's pre-death ritual consists of the things they would normally do in real life, but with the macabre knowledge that it will be the last time they do it; one final taste of the banality of humankind.

Brushing their teeth, shaving, smoking one final cigarette; maybe with tears in their eyes, or perhaps smiling maniacally that their determination to rid themselves of this world has finally come to fruition.

Ichiro Watanabe, a 52-year-old businessman attempted to take his life in Aokigahara in 2011 but was found and revived by a passing group. Watanabe was taken to hospital and nurtured back to good health. The statements he later made regarding his motivation for suicide is a revealing insight into why people feel compelled to resort to such extremes.

"It was the idea of having that one last cigarette and knowing I'd never have another one; that I'd never need another one. And the stub would be the only thing left of me. No work, no meetings, no stress, no early morning commutes, just blissful silence.

I always wondered whether people felt alone during and after their cigarette, or if they felt for the first time that they weren't alone. That instead they were in a forest where others had made the same hard decision that I was about to make.

That's the allure of Aokigahara: *to be able to commit suicide in the one place where it it's okay to end your life. You can be truly alone and there's no danger of your family having to find your dead body. That's certainly how it felt to me. The silence of the forest reassures you that it's okay to feel the way you do. It's ok, because others have ended their journey here, and nobody is judged for it.*

I think those people understood life would go on, with or without them; the world didn't need them there in order to keep turning. Someone deciding to end their life must see existence as something like watching a terrible movie that never ends. Their eyes keep being drawn to the exit sign that's blinking in the background, while everyone else in the cinema has their eyes glued to the screen. They know they can leave if they really want to, but before they do they have to convince themselves it's okay to leave. They've forgotten the movie from the moment they leave, but the movie continues to play. And it's the most subjective movie ever made – eliciting a different response in everyone who watches it.

It's a bit like the video tape in The Ring: after you watch it, you die. Well, we all die eventually, is that such a drag?"

This perception of life as a meaninglessness, monotonous inconvenience is a common theme amongst those who have left behind remnants of their philosophical beliefs in their wake. As previously mentioned, Japanese culture favours the "collective" over the individual, which can incite feelings of hatred towards the status quo. In turn, it is often found that the more anarchic suicide victims attempt to project their antagonism onto those they leave behind.

Andy Warhol once said the man's goal is not to live forever, but to create something that will. Most people interpret this as art; paintings, writings, music. But inside Aokigahara, a different picture is painted. There have been numerous incidents of people leaving behind objects they believe are cursed.

Japan has a native form of voodoo that dates back to the sixth century, if not previous. It seems the ceremony, called *ushi no koku mairi* is still being practiced. The act involves nailing the Japanese equivalent of a voodoo doll (*'wara ningyoo'*) to a "sacred tree" in order to bring harm to a person or persons.

These dolls have been found inside Aokigahara numerous times. While the forestry is not considered "sacred" by Japanese criteria, it can be argued that any tree which is the host of a swaying, dead body can be construed as important. A particular prominent image from the Aokigahara archives shows a cursed doll with a nailed through its chest upside down on a tree previously harbouring a suicide victim.

The dolls used are often made of straw. In some cases, children's dolls have been used, suggesting the perpetrator was hinting a world he feels has lost its innocence. The purpose of the doll is simply the catalyst to the inflicted curse, as it is the perpetrator's suicide which then imbues the doll with vengeful energy. Anyone who would then come into contact with the cursed possession is believed to be afflicted with the urge to join the dead.

These curses left upon the living world, then, can be viewed as desperate interpretations of art or a final insult to a world a person happy to leave behind. The sight of an upside down figurine in mock suicide shows a discernible contempt for a societal norms, and is perhaps their introverted way of trying to educate the rest of the world who don't see life through the same lens.

Souls of Unrest

Most people are familiar with the clichéd image of a Japanese ghost girl made famous by horror films such as The Grudge and The Ring. She is usually ghostly white with her face covered with black hair, dressed in rags and has black, soulless eyes. This image was not created specifically for movies, but was based on the centuries-old archetypal image of what a restless Japanese spirit is reported to look like.

These spirits, known as *Yūrei,* are said to haunt Aokigahara in large numbers, particularly at Japan's witching hour – between 2 and 3am. This is point at which the veil between our world and spiritual realm is at its most fragile, allowing ghosts and demons to pass freely into the physical world.

In order to understand the *Yūrei* fully, we must understand traditional Japanese beliefs about the afterlife. *Shinto* (the faith of the Japanese people) doesn't have heaven or hell the same way the Western world does. When a person dies, their soul leaves the body and enters a kind of purgatory. When the proper funeral rites are performed, the soul can go to the ancestors and thus become a protective spirit. However, if a person dies in a sudden, abnormal, or cruel manner, their spirit will instinctively turn into a *Yūrei.*

Additionally, it is also believed that if a person's body isn't buried with the ceremonial rights it deserves, or if a person dies while still suppressing strong negative emotions such as depression, rage or resentment, they would also become a *Yūrei.*

The Yūrei are believed to seek revenge against those who wronged them in life, and little can be done to stop this crusade. They will only disappear when their need for vengeance is satisfied, either by the spirit itself, or its family members. Sometimes, the Yūrei may haunt a lover until its passion is sated. In some cases, a *Shinto* or Buddhist priest may be successful in exorcising the spirit, but usually the Yūrei are unstoppable until they achieve their goals.

All three of these aspects; unnatural death, supressed rage, and improper funerary rites are routinely reported to occur in Aokigahara. And indeed, many of them can occur in *the same* person.

Suicide is a considered a sudden and unnatural way to die, with the majority of the suicide victims concealing an inner rage for a society which offered them so little. Official statements also confirm that many suicide victims' bodies are never found due to decomposition caused by the elements, or even get eaten by wild animals, meaning they are never given an appropriate burial.

Naturally, Aokigahara is considered the most haunted location in all of Japan. Many paranormal researchers have dubbed it the *Purgatory of Yūrei,* as they are believed to linger around the Suicide Forest indefinitely and exist only to inflict misery on those who enter their territory. Forest rangers, who have the arduous task of having to sift through the forest on a regular basis looking for corpses, claim to regularly hear high-pitched screams in a forest which is otherwise unnaturally silent. Hikers often report seeing objects moving and seeing shadows amongst the trees, and many people claim that looking directly at trees during the witching hour reveals the faces of the dead in the tree bark.

Over the years, forest officials have devised a respectful way to treat the corpses they discover on their regular walkthroughs in order to avoid them suffering a dishonourable death. The forest workers will carry any bodies they find down to the nearest police station, where they're held in a special room used specifically to house suicide corpses.

To prevent these souls from becoming a *Yūrei*, an officer will sleep in the same room as the corpse until the next morning. The reason for these strange sleeping arrangements is that it is believed if the corpse is left alone, it's very bad luck for the ghost of the suicide victim. Their spirits are said to scream throughout the night if left alone, and their bodies will get up and shuffle around, searching for company.

The Old Man And The Girl

In 2002, Mike Owen, a journalist for a British tabloid visited Aokigahara for research for a newspaper piece about the legacy of the Suicide Forest. He spent two days there in total, exploring as much of the forest as was possible and spoke to as many locals as he could. On the evening of his second day there, Owen reportedly heard a deafening scream coming from one of the caves below the ground.

Owen followed the source of the sound which eventually brought him to a large hole covered with moss, leaves and tree branches. Aokigahara plays host to hundreds of underground caves due to the way in which it was formed, although many of these sections are unreachable due to there being no way in.

What Owen saw inside the cave terrified him. He had heard ghost sightings were common but assumed they were simply exaggerated folk tales. What Owen saw in the cave was the ghostly outline of an elderly gentleman holding hands with a young girl. They both stared straight at him. With Owen too scared to avert his eyes, he watched them turn around and eventually walked further into the cave and out of sight.

Owen fled the forest quite quickly, unsure of what he had seen. When he returned to England, his newspaper article mentioned the ghostly incident, however it was largely considered a ruse in order to get people to visit the forest for tourist purposes.

Owen, being a reputable, veteran journalist took to investigating what may have happened. He had considered it was perhaps a hallucination, or they were in fact real people down in the cave, possibly forest workers.

However, Owen was contacted by several Japanese locals who had heard of previous sightings of the old man and the little girl. He had his doubts regarding the authenticity of these claims, however there was one detail which he failed to mention in his newspaper article; he never said the location where he saw them.

Sure enough, all sightings of the old man and the little girl took place in the same cave he saw them.

One year later in 2003, Owen received a newspaper clipping of an article in a Japanese newspaper. Unfortunately, he couldn't make out the contents as it was written in Japanese, however the main image showed an elderly gentleman sitting on a wooden chair with a young girl on his lap. Beside them, there was a middle aged man and woman who Owen presumed to be the parents of the girl in question. Additionally, the faces of the parents in the photograph had been crossed out.

Owen took the article to a translator at his workplace who gave a rough outline of what the article was about. It told a depressing, heartbreaking story.

Hitoshi and Kana Nakanishi, a Japanese couple, had been forced to move in with Kana's elderly father due to financial struggles. The pair were broke and unemployable due to run ins with the law, and were unable to properly raise their 6-year-old daughter Kurenai with the effort she deserved. Additionally, Kana's father (his name has been lost in translation) was sick and affording his healthcare was becoming problematic for the couple.

In order to solve their financial woes, Hitoshi and Kana Nakanishi hatched a plan.

Japanese governments are very lax when it comes to paying out for the deaths of people, especially suicides. Hitoshi and Kana Nakanishi planned to fake the suicide of Kana's father in order to fix their problems.

On an August afternoon in 2001, all four members of the Nakanishi family paid a visit to Aokigahara under the pretence of a road trip. They filled Kurenai's backpack with all of the necessary items in order to fake Kana's father's suicide. It included a bottle of whiskey, sleeping pills and a copy of *The Complete Manual of Suicide.*

The Nakanishi's plan was simple: send Kana's father and Kurenai into the depths of the forest, then get Kurenai to leave him there. It would echo the ancient practice of *ubasute*. The Nakanishi's told their daughter it was a game and that her grandfather would return in a few weeks' time, by which point they would have received their insurance money and could move out of his house. They would then lie about his whereabouts to Kurenai who they assumed would simply forget he existed as she grew older.

Hitoshi and Kana Nakanishi waited in their car as Kurenai and Kana's father walked into Aokigahara. Both were under the impression they would be playing a game of *onigokko* ('tag'). When they reached a suitable destination, Kurenai passed her grandfather a drink from her flask (as per instructions from her parents). He assumed it to be water, however it was actually mixed alcohol, which, in his already-weakened state, forced him to collapse due to the shock on his body.

Kurenai was told this would happen, which she believed to be 'normal'. She then ditched the contents of her backpack near to where her grandfather collapsed and ran back to her parents.

However, Kurenai noticed something in her backpack contents which she had forgotten about. Her parents had packed her some red tape which she was told to wrap around a tree on her entrance to the forest in order to find her way back. She hadn't.

Kurenai had gone so far into the forest that she couldn't remember her way back. She tried to backtrack but simply ended up further inside Aokigahara. Dusk was beginning to set in and she started to get upset. In her haste she began running through the forest as fast as possible to find someone.

Kurenai slipped on an uneven surface of the forest floor and fell down. She hit her head on a rock and passed out.

Her parents became concerned and eventually went in to look for her. However, Kurenai or her grandfather was never seen again. The only remains of them ever discovered by officials were Kurenai's backpack.

The story received little coverage in the Japanese media due to it dealing with several taboo subjects; suicide, missing children, child abuse and fraud. Further investigation would require legal action to be taken against both Hitoshi and Kana Nakanishi, whereas on the surface it can be construed as simply another two suicides inside Aokigahara. The Nakanishis confessed to their plans when authorities inquired as to the whereabouts of their daughter.

Mike Owen went on to report this incident in Britain, which encouraged paranormal enthusiasts to seek out these spectral apparitions for themselves. The haunting figure of these two neglected family members continue to be spotted in the Suicide Forest, always around the cave where Mike Owen claims to have seen them (and theorised to be the portion of rock which Kurenai died upon), always holding hands, together in death forever.

Kaidan

Scattered throughout Aokigahara are signs of caution to anyone there with suicidal tendencies. At the entrance of the designated trail into the forest a sign declares:

"Your life is a precious gift given to you by your parents. Please think about your parents, your brothers and sisters, to your children. Do not keep everything to yourself, talk about your problems. Do not be troubled alone."

There are additional heeds of warning further down the trail: *"Please reconsider,"* and *"Please consult the police before you decide to take your life."*

These three signs in particular had been placed by forest officials who are doing all they can within their power, albeit unsuccessfully, to prevent suicides. Locals have taken to this act of kindness with their own signs and messages of hope nailed to trees and propped up in the soil.

A quote regarding the exploration of life by Henry David Thoreau lies further down the designated trail:

"I went to the woods because I wished to live deliberately, to front only the essential facts of life, and see if I could not learn what it had to teach, and not, when I came to die, discover that I had not lived."

However, the woods have such a reputation that these minor deterrents do little to stop those determined to never leave. While people without suicidal thoughts are able to see the aesthetic beauty of Aokigahara in spite of its haunting legacy, those with a more pessimistic outlook see beauty in melancholy. Their whole perception of the forest will be illuminated by the *finality* of their intentions.

A case of revived suicide attempt in 2012 highlighted the perceptions between those without suicidal thoughts and those who had lost all will to exist. Junichi Tanaka, a 29-year-old male who was found in a tent on a December evening after attempting to poison himself, said that he felt everything in the forest drove him to end his life there. The signs, he believed, did not tell him to think of his family at all. Instead, they urged him to kill himself with messages about how he would not be missed by anyone and that everything he had achieved in life would be forgotten about in time.

There are, of course, no official signs making such statements, and was likely Tanaka's delusional state of mind skewing his perception of reality. However, in an eastern clearing of Aokigahara there is a makeshift gravestone with a message carved into its surface.

"Death is the milestone to which we value mortality. We wait for him like we await an old friend, often attempting to delay his intervention, but never to defy him entirely."

Many people have claimed to have found this gravestone, including Junichi Tanaka. In fact, Tanaka claims it was the site of this message which sealed his intentions to commit suicide. His tent was also discovered very close to its location. Despite Tanaka's possible delusions, others have discovered the gravestone and a few people have expressed outrage at its message.

A lone figure is said to appear at the sight of the gravestone during the early hours of the morning. The figure is of a lone man who simply sits at the gravestone until dawn, and then disperses. Unlike the vengeful spirit of the *Yūrei,* the man appears to emanate spectral rays of black light as opposed to a white, ghostly presence. No eyewitnesses have ever reported him to attack, or flee. He simply sits aside this nameless grave and waits.

The earliest report of this figure dates as far back as the 1960s, before Aokigahara's reputation as a death site was cemented. The message portrayed on the gravestone does not appear to be verbatim from any specific quotation or text, however, the words are very similar to the opening paragraph of a text dealing with Japanese folklore published in 1927, and allows speculation regarding the ghost's identity and what his particular obsession with this gravesite may be.

The text, entitled *'Kaidan'* (*Kai* – *'strange, mysterious, rare or bewitching apparition'*, *Dan* – *'talk' or 'recited narrative'*) included a folk tale dealing with a man coming to terms with the loss of his wife.

Kentarō was only a young man when he landed his first job as a prison guard. Prisons during the era of the story were simply cages in desolate areas of villages, watched over by a select few people. There was no judicial system to speak of. Torture and execution of prisoners was an everyday occurrence, and Kentarō was the person to administer them.

At age 16, Kentarō was forced to behead prisoners when they became an inconvenience. By 18, he had executed over 50 criminals. He learnt where to cut them so they died most efficiently. He learnt how to professionally hang criminals so that their death was quick and never failed. He became proficient in torture in order to extract information, many times administering so much pain that the prisoner died of extreme fatigue.

By 25, Kentarō was one of the most proficient executioners in Japan. His skills became widely known and his presence requested across the country. He was sent to a district in southeastern Japan to execute a woman by the name of Matsu who had been imprisoned for crimes of infidelity.

However, when the time came, Kentarō refused.

Kentarō claimed that Matsu was the most beautiful woman he had ever seen, and that he could not bring himself to murder her.

Several years passed of Kentarō's reluctance to take her life, for which Matsu was eternally grateful. However, the Japanese Emperor demanded her death as she no longer offered any use to him. He told Kentarō that if he didn't take her life, another executioner would take his place.

Kentarō agreed to end her life under one condition: that he could marry her on the day of her death. The Emperor agreed, and Kentarō and Matsu married in the forest at the base of Mount Fuji.

During their vows, Kentarō promised Matsu that they would meet again in death. They then kissed, and Kentarō wrapped a noose around Matu's neck and suffocated her as painlessly as he knew how.

The years went by. Kentarō became the most famous executioner in Japan. He earned a fortune from his profession, however all he longed for was his death day in order to see Matsu once more.

Kentarō retired at the age of 60. Not a day had gone by in which he didn't think of his estranged lover from thirty years previous. The years went by. Kentarō aged and aged, but death would not come for him.

At age 88, Kentarō tried to overdose on medication. However, he simply woke up the next morning unharmed.

At 94, Kentarō attempted to slice his heart from his chest, but his heart he felt still belonged to Matsu.

At 100, Kentarō travelled back to the site of his wife's death. A tree at the base of Mount Fuji. Kentarō attempted to hang himself, but each time, the rope would break.

As Kentarō lay on the soil after three failed suicide attempts, he was visited by an apparition in the forest. A deathly white figure. It told Kentarō that he was the luckiest man in the world.

Kentarō had become a Messenger of Death due to his life's work of execution and torment. And in return had been cursed with the affliction of eternal life. Kentarō had witnessed death so many times that he had become immune to its effects.

He would live forever.

Kentarō tried to tell the apparition that he didn't want this. He wanted to pass over to the next world. He had a promise to keep.

But the apparition faded away.

To this day, it seems that Kentarō has not given up on his promise of meeting the woman he loves once again. He seemingly sits atop her grave each and every night, waiting for Death to take him. No one knows how many years Kentarō has been waiting. The only thing that is certain is that Death never comes.

Red Child's Hand

Aokigahara's visual aesthetics cannot be denied. Despite its heritage, the Sea of Trees is an astoundingly beautiful landmark - even in the, shabby, overgrown state of recent times. Beauty and death have been naturally linked throughout history; from the Victorian practice of *memento mori* in which death is photographed and displayed, to modern enthusiasm for the macabre such as those who visit Aokigahara (and other notorious suicide locations) for the purposes of discovering dead bodies, morbid attraction is as present today than ever before.

This connection can be explored further still in regards to the notion of physical beauty. In 2011, student Kazuhiko Ohmae was visiting the Suicide Forest for tourist purposes when he claims to have witnessed something very bizarre.

"She was standing at the base of this huge tree – I think it was a honey locust tree – several miles deep into the advised [walking trail]. She was wearing this long, white flowing robe, like a wedding dress. From what I could see she was absolutely beautiful. She had black hair down to her waist and her eyes were solid blue. She had this glow, and it felt like it was saying… 'come to me', like it was dragging me closer. I walked slightly closer to her; the air was freezing cold around where she was standing. Her hair was blowing harshly in the wind but she just stood there, welcoming me.

When I was [within reasonable distance] of her – it was so weird – I felt this hand on my shoulder. I looked around and it was this bright red, bloodshot hand resting on me. I had no idea what was going on. I just fell to the ground. I think I passed out. Some passers-by nursed me back to health when they found me; they thought I had tried to kill myself but I had to explain to them I'd gone into shock. I don't think they believed me.

When I woke up, she was gone. I think I could see the beautiful lady's face in the tree bark if I looked hard enough but that might have just been my imagination."

Ohmae's tale has been reported to have occurred in the past, although not just in Aokigahara, but all across Japan. It is believed that such a phenomenon is attributed to the *akateko,* translated to English as 'red child's hand'.

The *akateko* is a form of *yōkai* (ghost, apparition) which appears as a severed hand hanging from a tree. It is often considered to have once belonged to a now-deceased child or infant due the hands usually being very small and unformed. There is not much known about the *akateko,* including where they originate from and what their purposes may be. Their appearances are also usually accompanied with sightings of beautiful spectral apparitions who attempt to allure their targets towards them, as with Ohmae's experience.

Some theories contemplate the notion of a mother and child who have both passed on who are simply causing mischief and misery to any unlucky passers-by. Reports of *akateko* experiences rarely result in injury or death, which gives weight to this idea of child's play. Given that the dismembered hands who fall on targets' shoulders are so small, this suggests that perhaps the child was never fully formed in the womb and may be an apparition symbolic of an unborn child.

Afterlife

It is said that the greatest motivator of all is love. Love is a unique force which remains largely a psychological and biological mystery to humankind. It can toy with our emotions and compel us to make decisions we would never make without such a powerful, alien force guiding our intentions.

Murder and suicides in the name of love are more common than we would like to admit, and is in fact the third most common reasons for taking one's own life after depression and financial woes. The classic tale of Romeo and Juliet remains relevant even four-hundred years after its publication, showing that love and suicide are still a common pairing in the modern world.

A particularly bleak tale of a woman whose body was found in Aokigahara in 2004 deals with the subject of love and loss, as well as being grounded in religious morals; a further common factor amongst suicide victims.

25-year-old Sakuko Iwasaki was reported missing in late 2003 by her parents after leaving for college and never returning. In February 2004, her belongings were found in the Suicide Forest by park rangers and were traced back to Iwasaki via her college books. Iwasaka's parents reported that their daughter struggled with depression and anxiety but was able to control her emotions through religious healing. Her parents were active Catholics (a rarity in Japan), and urged Sakuko to also follow in their beliefs.

As previously mentioned, Christianity or Catholicism are not widely practiced in Japan; something which attributes to Japan's perception of suicide being deemed heroic. There is said to be around 500,000 practicing Catholics in Japan; less than 1% of the population. Those that do practice

Catholicism do so in the same way as their Western counterparts.

Sakuko Iwasaki would visit a practicing Catholic priest in her home city of Yamagata (around 500kms away from Aokigahara) every two weeks and talk to him about her life, her feelings, her problems. The priest, Rev. Yamakawa of the Yamagata Catholic Church, would sit and listen to Iwasaki talk for hours at a time. Iwasaki had only one or two friends due to her mental struggles. She chose to keep herself isolated as much as she could due to her perception that the outside world was a dangerous place to live and would be increasingly unkind to her. Rev. Yamakawa was her only outlet for her true intentions.

Iwasaki told of her suicidal thoughts to Yamakawa on several occasions, but Yamakawa would continually reassure her that there was no need to take her own life.

He would tell her she was young and had much to live for, and that the world is lucky to have such a beautiful, talented young lady in its midst. On one occasion in the winter of 2003, Iwasaki broke down into tears in Rev. Yamakawa's church and as she cried in his arms, she told him that she had romantic feelings for him. Iwasaki felt that he was her rock, and was the only person who understood her.

Unfortunately, Rev Yamakawa would not return Iwasaki's infatuation. Both morally and religiously, Yamakawa felt it would not be a wise idea, even for the sake of her psychological benefit. Indeed, all reports claim that Iwasaki was a beautiful, albeit slightly troubled young lady, but Yamakawa stood his professional and faithful ground.

This would be the last time Yamakawa, or anyone, would ever see Sakuko Iwasaki alive. The morning after she disappeared she was officially reported missing, although both her parents and Rev. Yamakawa knew that she had likely taken her own life. Yamakawa would go on to say that her suicide "was inevitable" and that "no amount of religious healing could keep her on this earth". It would not be for another three months before she was discovered 600 kilometres away, buried beneath leaves and soil in the Sea of Trees after drowning herself with pills and alcohol.

It was only though Sakuko Iwasaki's possessions that authorities could determine her identity. She had decomposed quite significantly due to the harsh winter conditions, leaving only her clothes and backpack in her wake.

Iwasaki's details were easily discovered from documents in her backpack; name, address, university attended, but authorities also found a book of hymns belonging to the

Yamagata Catholic Church. The book was found a short distance from her body, suggesting it was in her hands at the time of her death. On the first page of the book was a handwritten note from Rev. Yamakawa telling her to "never give up, never walk away" (roughly translated from Japanese), but it seems that this wasn't enough to keep Iwasaki's demons at bay.

Iwasaki's suicide was a devastating blow for Yamakawa, despite his beliefs that she would eventually succumb to her troubles. It took its toll on him quite significantly as he felt as though he had failed in his duty of care to those in need. He would later admit that he felt entirely responsible for Iwasaki's death due to his rejection of her love for him. His faith prevented them ever being anything other than Listener and Speaker; a dilemma which would haunt Yamakawa's conscience until his own death in 2005.

Conclusion

It is said that a backdrop of forestry can make even the bleakest images beautiful, and Aokigahara may prove this more than anywhere else on earth.

In many respects, and as stories in this volume may prove, it is not the Suicide Forest itself which is melancholic, but the tragic backstory of those who choose to dwell there eternally. It could even be considered that the existence of Aokigahara can be a macabre form of relief and comfort to some. *No matter how bad the struggles of life become, the Suicide Forest will offer a way out.*

It is truly a haunting, hellish location, and one imbued with an almost supernatural allure. We must remember, however, that the happenings inside Aokigahara are not to be spoken lightly of. They are dreadful, often-avoidable events which need not be romanticised or intensified.

Aokigahara remains as prominent as ever at the time of writing. Many actions have been taken to limit the deathly occurrences which are so commonplace in the forest, albeit with varying degrees of success. It is unlikely that the unnatural death rate inside Aokigahara will be severely reduced any time soon, and is nigh on impossible for it to ever disassociate itself from being an open air asylum for the unsettled spirits of this world and the next.

Whether it be the sight of a decayed corpses still wearing the brand name clothes they passed away in, the discarded possessions of those without the will to exist, or the sight of frequent spectral apparitions, there is hardly a soul on earth who wouldn't be unnerved by *something* in the Suicide Forest.

21525363R00065

Printed in Great Britain
by Amazon